MEL
GIBSON

by
Jill C. Wheeler

Visit us at
www.abdopub.com

Published by ABDO & Daughters, an imprint of ABDO
Publishing Company, 4940 Viking Drive, Edina, MN 55435.
Copyright ©2003 by Abdo Consulting Group, Inc.
International copyrights reserved in all countries. No part of
this book may be reproduced in any form without written
permission from the publisher.

Printed in the United States.

Graphic Design: John Hamilton
Cover Design: Mighty Media
Cover photo: Corbis
Interior photos: AP/Wide World, p. 6, 21, 22-23, 26, 33, 37,
40, 43, 45, 48, 50-51, 53, 56, 59
    Corbis, p. 1, 5, 9, 11, 12-13, 14, 17, 18, 25, 29, 31, 34, 39,
        47, 55, 57, 60-61
    MGM, p. 38
    Orion Pictures Corp., p. 27, 35
    Paramount Pictures, p. 32, 62
    Tristar Pictures, p. 44
    Warner Bros., p. 41, 49

Library of Congress Cataloging-in-Publication Data

Wheeler, Jill C., 1964-
    Mel Gibson / Jill C. Wheeler.
        p. cm. — (Star tracks)
    Includes index.
    Summary: Discusses the private life and stage and film
career of actor Mel Gibson.
ISBN 1-57765-767-5
        1. Gibson, Mel—Juvenile literature. 2. Motion picture
actors and actresses—Australia—Biography—Juvenile
literature. [1. Gibson, Mel. 2. Actors and actresses.] I. Title.
II. Series.

PN3018.G5 W49 2002
791.43'028'092—dc21
[B]
                                                2001045949

CONTENTS

Cast Clown 4

New York to Sydney 8

Actor by Accident 16

Mad Max 24

Aussie Star 30

Back to America 36

Riggs 42

The Director's Chair 46

And the Oscar Goes To 52

Still a Heartthrob 58

Glossary 63

Web Sites 63

Index 64

CAST
CLOWN

CAMERAS ARE ROLLING IN A SMALL summer cottage in Bayside, Maine. In the scene, a mother is serving lunch to her family from a steaming pan of pasta. Suddenly an alarm goes off, and the film's director jumps from behind the camera. "Everyone duck!" he yells, his index finger pointing like a gun. "Don't move! Wait for the bomb squad!"

The cast is silent until they realize someone has burned some of the Spaghetti Os being used for the scene and set off the smoke detector. "Oh Mel," sighs one of the young actors. "You're so silly."

It's just another day on the set of *The Man Without a Face*, directed by Mel Gibson. And for the actors and crew used to working with Gibson, it's business as usual. The 45-year-old actor is well known in Hollywood for his on-the-set pranks. He's been known to hire high school marching bands to serenade costars, or burp as loudly as he can after a tense, dramatic scene. Many of his friends call him "the fourth Stooge."

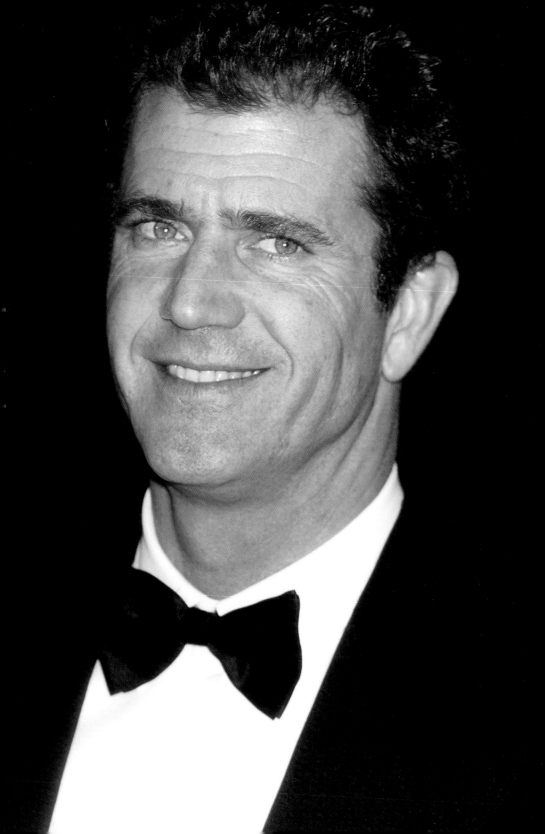

"Mel's like the class clown."

"Mel's like the class clown," says three-time costar René Russo. "He's like a hyperactive kid."

Gibson may generate the laughs, but he's serious about his work. He is one of the most successful actors in Hollywood. He is paid a reported $25 million for each film, which makes him the world's highest-paid actor. He is also a man of contrasts. He can move around a movie set humming his favorite opera tune or join his sons in a vicious paintball battle and be perfectly at ease doing either.

In a business known for broken marriages, Gibson has been married to the same woman for more than 20 years. He has surprised Hollywood coworkers with his conservative views on sensitive issues like birth control and capital punishment. He has also made tabloid headlines for drinking, brawling, and flirting with women. And while he's been called a chauvinist, Gibson has been known to donate money to battered women's shelters.

Gibson is also a very private person. "Mel is unfailingly courteous," says actress Linda Hunt, who worked with him early in his career. "Those beautiful blue eyes can take you right in, but at the same time they put up a barrier that keeps you from coming in too far."

NEW YORK
TO
SYDNEY

MEL COLUMCILLE GERARD GIBSON WAS born on January 3, 1956, in Peekskill, New York. He was the sixth of 10 children born to Hutton and Anne Gibson. Mel's parents later adopted one more child.

Hutton was a very religious man, just as his father had been. Hutton had studied for the priesthood as a young man, but then decided the Roman Catholic Church was becoming too liberal. After quitting seminary, he joined the army and served in the Pacific in World War II.

After the military, Hutton took a job as a brakeman for the New York Central Railroad. He moved his young family from New York City to upstate New York because he felt it was a better place to raise children. Eventually, the family moved to a small farm. Anne could not drive, so the family was isolated in their farmhouse while Hutton was away at work.

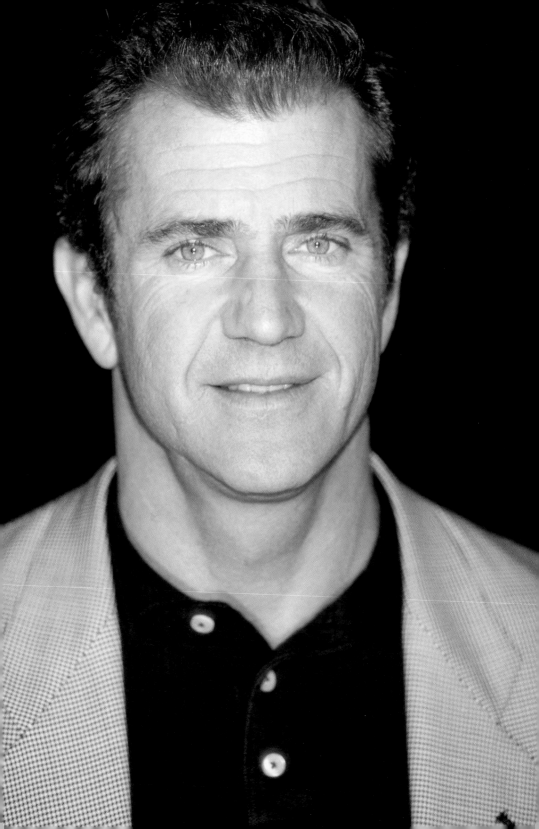

It was not an easy life. Hutton was a devout Catholic, and he insisted that his children be raised the same way. He had strict rules about behavior and morality. He told his children that they were never to smoke or drink. He also disapproved of couples getting too involved with one another before they were married.

The Gibson family did not have a lot of money. Mel and his siblings had to learn to entertain themselves. Mel and his brothers amused themselves by jumping off the roof of the family barn, and fighting each other. "We'd just about kill one another," Mel recalled. "Very satisfying." Even as a youngster, Mel had the mark of a rebel. He once stole the family car. Another time he stapled his sister's head.

In 1964, Hutton injured his back at work. The accident cost him his job. Since he was injured on the job and unable to work, Hutton sued the railroad for compensation. Meanwhile, Mel's older siblings got jobs to help pay the family's bills.

Even as a youngster, Mel had the mark of a rebel.

Hutton's legal case against the railroad lasted nearly four years. As the case dragged on, Hutton became increasingly unhappy. It was the late 1960s, and the United States was going through a period of rapid change. The war in Vietnam dragged on, accompanied by many protests. Drug use was increasing, as was sexual freedom. Hutton felt that people in the northeastern United States treated Catholics badly. All in all, he felt the country was headed toward moral ruin.

Mel Gibson arrives in Berlin for the German premiere of The Patriot, *July 10, 2000.*

In February 1968, the courts awarded Hutton
$145,000 for his injury. That same year, Hutton
won $21,000 on the TV quiz show *Jeopardy*. He
used the money to move his family to Australia,
his mother's homeland. He hoped Australia would
be a more moral place to finish raising his
children. Also, because Hutton was against the

*Mel Gibson at the
Hollywood premiere of*
What Women Want.

Vietnam War, he didn't want his sons drafted when they were only 18 years old. On the way to their new country, the family visited Ireland, Scotland, England, Rome, and the Vatican.

In November 1968, the family settled in a suburb north of Sydney, Australia. Twelve-year-old Mel was sent to St. Leo's College, a Catholic boys school. Mel didn't like school. The teachers at St. Leo's were very strict. Plus, Mel found himself being teased for his American accent and called a Yank. He quickly learned to fake an Australian accent.

Mel began to rebel against the authorities at St. Leo's. "I didn't like school—who does?" he said. "I got busted for smoking and wagging, which means you just leave, you go to a pool hall for the day. I was very good at that." Once Mel even competed with two friends to see who could get in the most trouble in a single day. Mel won—he was disciplined 27 times in one day.

After a while, Hutton decided St. Leo's wasn't teaching Mel enough about religion. He sent Mel to Asquith High School instead. Mel continued to play the rebel at school and was known as an entertainer among the other students. He also began taking an interest in girls, though he was very shy around them. In the classroom, his grades were simply average.

ACTOR
BY
ACCIDENT

AS HIS HIGH SCHOOL YEARS ENDED,
Gibson had to figure out what he wanted to do for
a career. At one time he had considered entering
the priesthood. By the time school finished, he had
given up on that idea. He considered becoming a
chef or a journalist, but nothing really jumped out
at him as the ideal career. In the meantime he took
odd jobs, including bagging groceries and waxing
surfboards.

Gibson didn't know it, but his sister Mary
thought he would make a good actor. She had
always enjoyed his tricks and practical jokes.
Without telling him, she filled out an application
form to the National Institute of Dramatic Arts
(NIDA) at the University of New South Wales in
Sydney. She sent it in with his photo and five
dollars. Then she waited.

Gibson was working at an orange juice bottling plant when he learned NIDA was interested in him. He didn't like working at the factory, so he decided to try acting. Gibson beat out a number of other students competing for slots at NIDA and began taking courses in 1974.

Some of the classes at NIDA were very hard. For example, he would have to play a character experiencing strong emotions while standing in front of a crowd of teachers and students. It was a tough thing to do. Gibson later said it had helped that he'd had to pretend for so many years to be something he wasn't while at school.

Gibson took a casual approach to his classes at NIDA. Some of the other students desperately wanted to be actors. They resented him for being less committed to acting. Once, a teacher almost threw Gibson out of class because he refused to participate in an exercise that he said was a waste of his time.

After a year at NIDA, Gibson moved away from home and found a place with three friends. Their home quickly became a place for parties. Gibson also began to shine at NIDA.

Gibson won the lead in the school's production of *Romeo & Juliet*. He said his first acting experience was frightening. "My first time on stage I almost lost my lunch," he said. "I was terrified. But the more you do it, the easier it gets." As time went on, Gibson earned more roles. No matter what character he played, his charisma seemed to entrance audiences. When he cut his hair and beard for a play he began getting noticed for his good looks, too.

In November 1976, Gibson had his first opportunity outside NIDA. He was offered a role in a low-budget surfing film called *Summer City*. He earned $400 for his part, the minimum wage for an acting job. Because the movie had such a small budget, Gibson and the other actors had to help out with many aspects of the production. It was a great education for him, teaching him about what went into making a movie.

Gibson then got a job on an Australian soap opera. He quickly decided he didn't like working in television. TV shows have to be done quickly, so there isn't always time to do things the way they could best be done.

His next job was with the South Australian Theatre Company. This gave Gibson the chance to work on a stage production of *Waiting for Godot*. Like many actors, Gibson enjoyed stage work. It gave him the chance to see and feel the audience's reaction immediately. In a movie, actors don't know how the audience will react until months later.

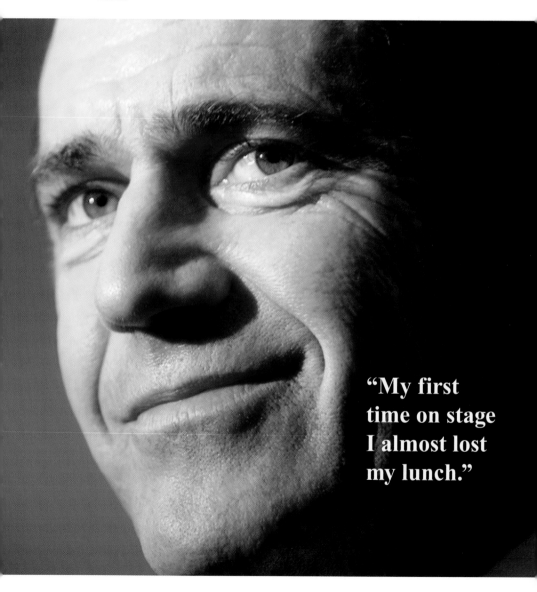

"My first time on stage I almost lost my lunch."

The theater company performed for awhile in Adelaide, Australia. While there, Gibson met a young woman named Robyn Moore. She was a dental assistant and was renting a room in the same house Gibson was staying at. Moore had a boyfriend at the time, so they just became friends. "It wasn't love at first sight," Gibson explained. "We were just platonic friends. In fact, I think she thought I was kind of obnoxious."

Mel Gibson, right, with fellow Australian actor Geoffrey Rush in Waiting for Godot.

MAD
MAX

GIBSON GRADUATED FROM NIDA IN
October 1977. Even before his graduation, he had
lined up his next project. A well-known Australian
talent agent named Bill Shannahan had seen
Gibson's work in *Summer City*.

Shannahan had lined up the soap opera
appearance for Gibson and alerted others to the
promising young actor. In September 1977, he
approached Gibson about taking a role in a new
movie directed by Dr. George Miller. It was to be
called *Mad Max*.

Just before Gibson auditioned for the role, he
wound up in a fierce bar fight. The fight left his
face a mess. "I had stitches in my head. I couldn't
see," Gibson told a reporter. The bruised and
battered look was just what Miller had in mind for
the loner cop in *Mad Max*, and Gibson got the job.

**More offers came
Gibson's way
after the success
of *Mad Max*.**

Mad Max is a dark and violent tale of society after the next world war. Many people criticized the film for its violence. In fact, some of the actors were real-life members of the infamous Hell's Angels motorcycle gang. The film didn't do well in the United States, but it was the biggest money-making film in Australia in 1979. It also earned Gibson a Best Actor Award from the Australian Film Institute.

More offers came Gibson's way after the success of *Mad Max*. He returned to the stage for *Oedipus Rex* and *Henry IV*. He then took the lead in a small film called *Tim*, in which he played a mentally retarded gardener. Unlike *Mad Max*, *Tim* gave Gibson a chance to demonstrate more depth in a character. The work earned him another Best Actor Award from the Australian Film Institute.

Gibson's next project was a war movie called *Attack Force Z*. It was shot on location in Taiwan. Production on the film was a headache for Gibson and his costar, New Zealand actor Sam Neill. The film's director was replaced after the actors had already agreed to do the project. Gibson didn't like the new director. He voiced his dislike and drowned his sorrows in alcohol during the shoot. The movie received good reviews, yet it was never shown in the United States. After that, Gibson decided to say no to any more low-budget films.

Gibson and Robyn Moore had started dating not long after they met. On June 7, 1980, they were married. After a brief honeymoon, Gibson accepted another TV job. It was a part on an Australian prison drama called *Punishment*. Gibson disliked the long hours and tight deadlines of TV. Fortunately, he was asked to star in a film by Australian director Peter Weir, called *Gallipoli*. Gibson's days in TV were over.

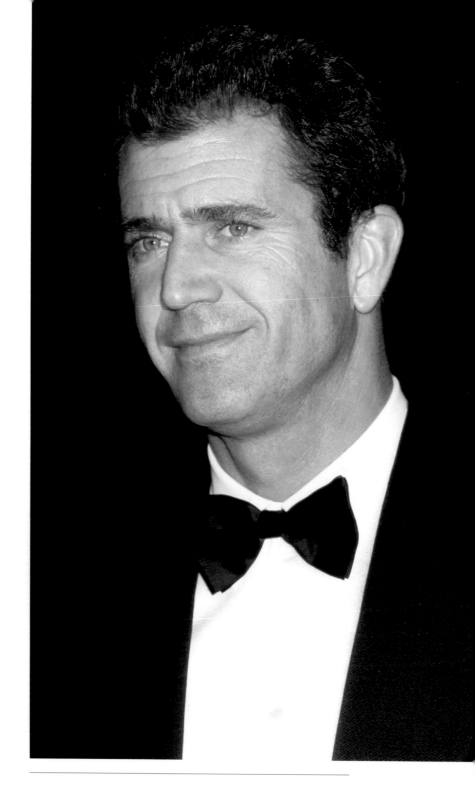

AUSSIE

STAR

THE GALLIPOLI CAMPAIGN WAS A LAND and sea operation during World War I. In the campaign, British, French, Australian, and New Zealand forces attempted to invade the Ottoman Empire, which was centered in what is now the country of Turkey. The action occurred near the Gallipoli Peninsula near Istanbul, Turkey. More than 200,000 soldiers, including many Australians and New Zealanders, died in the unsuccessful effort.

Filming the movie *Gallipoli* was difficult. Gibson and the rest of the cast and crew endured blistering heat and bitter cold while filming in Australia and Egypt. While Gibson was in Egypt, Moore gave birth to their first child. They named her Hannah.

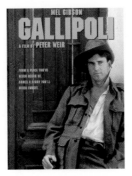

Gallipoli earned good reviews and gave Gibson his third Best Actor Award from the Australian Film Institute. He followed that movie with a sequel to *Mad Max* titled *The Road Warrior* in 1981. Like the first *Mad Max*, this one was nonstop action and heavy on violence. Gibson again played the law enforcer, Max. The sequel went on to make more money than the original.

Weir signed Gibson for his next project, *The Year of Living Dangerously*. The movie is a story about a journalist who has a love affair with a British diplomat during a turbulent time in Indonesia. The film gave Gibson a chance to play something other than a law enforcer. The 5-foot-10-inch actor had to wear lifts in his shoes to appear as tall as his costar, Sigourney Weaver. The movie was filmed in the Philippines and then in Australia. The last location meant Gibson could be on hand for the birth of his second and third children. Twins Edward and Christian were born in June 1982.

In the fall of 1982, Gibson returned to live theater to act in a production of *Death of a Salesman* in Sydney. He turned down several roles in Hollywood that would have made him a lot of money. Instead, he and his family were getting settled on their ranch in northern Victoria, Australia.

Gibson went in front of the camera again to play Fletcher Christian for 1984's *The Bounty*. The movie told the story of the British merchant ship *Bounty*. Christian was the first mate who led the mutiny against  Captain William Bligh in 1789. The movie was a remake of the original 1935 film on the incident.

Filming for *The Bounty* was on an island near Tahiti. The island was a tropical paradise, but spending four months somewhere so remote was difficult. Many people criticized Gibson's behavior on the set. The film itself didn't do well. Critics said it didn't live up to the original *Mutiny on the Bounty*.

BACK
TO
AMERICA

BY THIS TIME GIBSON WAS GETTING noticed. His good looks and acting ability already had people comparing him to John Wayne and Harrison Ford. Hollywood was calling. His first American movie was *The River*, costarring Sissy Spacek. Gibson's keen ear for accents made it no problem for the transplanted Aussie to sound like a Tennessee farmer.

Following *The River*, Gibson traveled to Toronto, Canada, to film *Mrs. Soffel* with Diane Keaton. Like several of his other films, the shooting conditions were unpleasant. And like other times, Gibson turned to alcohol to get through.

In just a few years, Gibson had gone from an unknown to a man on the verge of stardom. He now had four children but was rarely able to see them. The near constant travel and celebrity status were taking their toll. At age 27, he confided to a reporter, "Everything's just been happening too fast. I've gotta put the brakes on here or I'll smack into something."

That's exactly what happened to him while filming *Mrs. Soffel*. Gibson was driving drunk when he ran a red light and collided with another car. The police arrested him and fined him $300. Even worse, as far as Gibson was concerned, his wife was very upset with him. But he kept on drinking.

The Bounty, *The River*, and *Mrs. Soffel* all were released in 1984. Gibson immediately went to work on the third part in the Mad Max series. *Mad Max: Beyond Thunderdome* was the first of the Mad Max movies to be filmed with a relatively big budget. It was filmed in the Australian outback in temperatures so high several crew members suffered heat exhaustion. Gibson again turned to alcohol to cope with the rough conditions. Some said he would drink five beers before filming started, and more later in the day.

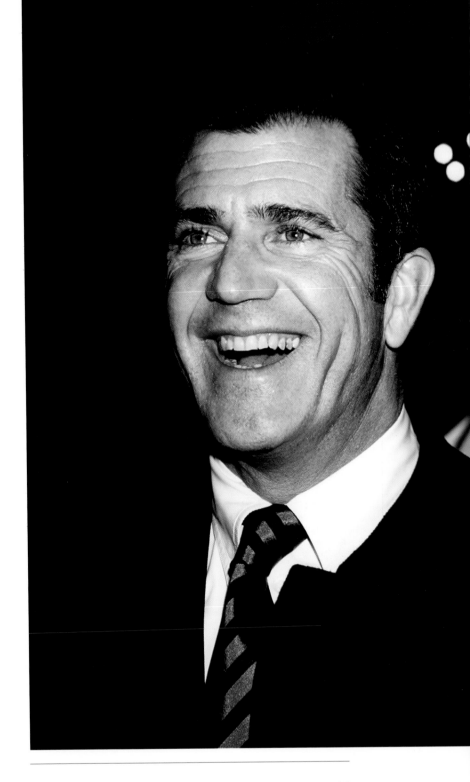

Mel Gibson and Julia Roberts at the world premiere of Conspiracy Theory *in Los Angeles, August 4, 1997.*

MEL GIBSON
MAD MAX
BEYOND THUNDERDOME

Tina Turner, Gibson's costar in *Beyond Thunderdome*, spotted his alcohol problem. While filming, she wrote, "Don't screw this up" on a photo of Gibson and sent it to him. "She was a woman of far greater experience than myself," Gibson recalled. "It really made me stop and think."

After *Beyond Thunderdome*, Gibson took 18 months off. He retreated to the family ranch in Australia to spend time with his family. While at home, Gibson drank less. Instead, he tended his 200 head of cattle and rebuilt a cottage with his father. Though out of sight, he certainly wasn't out of mind. In 1985, *People* magazine named him their first ever Sexiest Man Alive. Gibson later joked about the honor, "That implies there are a lot of dead guys who got more points than I did."

RIGGS

IN 1987, A RESTED GIBSON WAS READY TO take on Hollywood. He returned to the screen in the 1987 hit *Lethal Weapon*. *Lethal Weapon* featured Gibson as Marty Riggs, the impulsive partner to Danny Glover's experienced Roger Murtaugh. Gibson enjoyed the part. He also felt fortunate that his family could join him in Hollywood for the filming. In 1998, the Gibson family added a fifth child, Louis.

Lethal Weapon cleaned up at the box office. Almost overnight, Gibson became a star in America as well as Australia. Hollywood's celebrity status was hard on Gibson, however. He started drinking again soon after his family returned to Australia. Rumors began about him spending time with other women. When he started reading those rumors in the newspaper, Gibson decided it was time to quit drinking. He joined his family in Australia, though not for long. Hollywood wanted him back.

Mel Gibson in
Lethal Weapon.

Gibson again began making back-to-back movies. In 1988, he played a reformed drug dealer in the movie *Tequila Sunrise*. *Tequila Sunrise* paired him with actor Kurt Russell. The two became friends and came up with another movie idea to star Gibson along with Russell's longtime partner, Goldie Hawn. That resulted in 1990's *Bird on a Wire*. Before *Bird on a Wire*, Gibson repeated the role of Riggs for the successful sequel *Lethal Weapon 2*.

In early 1990, Gibson also filmed *Air America*. The movie was shot in northern Thailand and Laos. Once again, the Gibson family joined him on location and filming went smoothly. Then Moore returned to Australia to give birth to the couple's sixth child, Milo. Gibson began drinking again and showed a bad temper to other crew members. He was glad when the filming was over and he could return home to his wife and children.

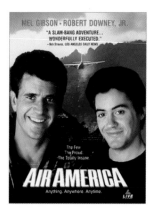

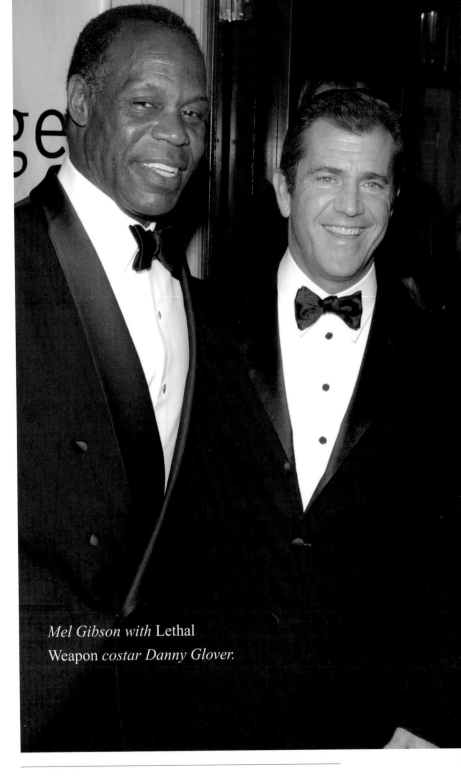

Mel Gibson with Lethal Weapon *costar Danny Glover.*

THE DIRECTOR'S CHAIR

FOLLOWING *AIR AMERICA*, GIBSON'S career took a turn. Director Franco Zeffirelli approached him about a starring role in a new movie version of the play *Hamlet,* by William Shakespeare. Unlike his past action-hero roles, the part of Hamlet would be almost entirely dialogue. Plus, Gibson would be starring with a cast of actors and actresses already famous for their dramatic talents.

Hollywood was incredulous when Zeffirelli announced his leading man. Few people knew Gibson had begun his career on the stage and they questioned his ability. After the film was released even critics agreed Mel Gibson was more than handsome. He was also talented.

Gibson's mother never saw his performance in *Hamlet*. She died in December 1990, shortly before the film was released.

Mel Gibson receives an award from the American Museum of the Moving Image, March 7, 2002, in New York City.

After *Hamlet*, Gibson signed a four-movie contract with Warner Bros. He also listened to his wife and his friends, who feared his alcohol problem would harm his career. In mid-1991, Gibson's wife convinced him to get help from Alcoholics Anonymous (AA).

The first step for someone seeking help from AA is to admit they have a problem with alcohol. "I realized that I had used alcohol as a prop," Gibson said about his experiences during those years. "I'd missed out on the joys of being a parent." Since then, Gibson has overcome his drinking problem.

In 1992, Gibson starred in *Lethal Weapon 3* and *Forever Young*. Like the other *Lethal Weapon* movies, *Lethal Weapon 3* was successful. Yet by this time, Gibson was ready to play someone other than Riggs. In fact, he wanted to try his hand at directing.

For his directing debut, Gibson turned to the book *The Man Without a Face*. It is the story of a reclusive former teacher whose face was horribly scarred in a fire. The book captivated him. "In my business, we're judged on appearances first," Gibson told a reporter. "My movie is about looking past appearances to test the real worth of people."

Originally, Gibson wanted someone else to play the lead role, but no one would take it. "I was my fourth choice for that role," he joked. He took it reluctantly, and it was exhausting for him to both direct and act. When it was done, critics said Gibson's directorial debut was promising.

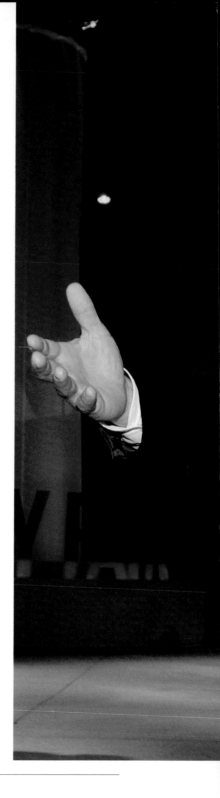

Mel Gibson arrives at the
Vanity Fair *Oscar party,*
March 24, 2002, in West
Hollywood, California.

AND THE
OSCAR
GOES TO...

HAMLET AND *THE MAN WITHOUT A FACE* had both been serious dramas. Next, Gibson wanted to realize another long-held desire—he wanted to act in a western. He got the chance with *Maverick* in 1994. *Maverick* was a comedy that paired him with James Garner and Jodie Foster. It was based on the 1960s TV show of the same name.

In 1994, Gibson returned to the director's chair to film, coproduce, and star in the epic film *Braveheart*. *Braveheart* was based on the life of 13th-century Scottish rebel William Wallace. Wallace is a legend in Scotland for his bravery in fighting the English. The film resulted in Gibson's first Academy Awards, or Oscars. He received one Oscar for best director and one for best picture. He also received a Golden Globe Award for best picture.

Mel Gibson holds his two Oscars for Braveheart *at the 68th Annual Academy Awards in Los Angeles, March 25, 1996. He won for Best Director and Best Film.*

Gibson's next movie was *Ransom*. *Ransom* was about a married couple whose son is kidnapped. For costar René Russo, the topic was emotionally exhausting. Gibson, however, managed to lighten the mood on the set after filming. "Mel would burp as loud as he could," Russo said. "There's a joy and abandon when he plays. He's like a child in some ways."

Gibson's childlike side showed up again while filming *Conspiracy Theory*. He sent costar Julia Roberts a gift-wrapped, freeze-dried rat. "I didn't know she had a phobia about rats," he said later. "She screamed her head off. It was kind of gratifying."

Gibson continued working almost nonstop. In 1998, he starred in *Lethal Weapon 4*, and in 1999, he played a thief in *Payback*. The birth of the Gibson's seventh child, Tommy, also occurred in 1999. While Tommy was too young to notice, other children enjoyed Gibson's voice work in *Chicken Run* in 2000. It was the second time he'd done voice work for a children's film. He was also the voice of John Smith in Disney's *Pocahontas*. "After all my hard work," said Gibson, "I'm finally cool in my kids' eyes."

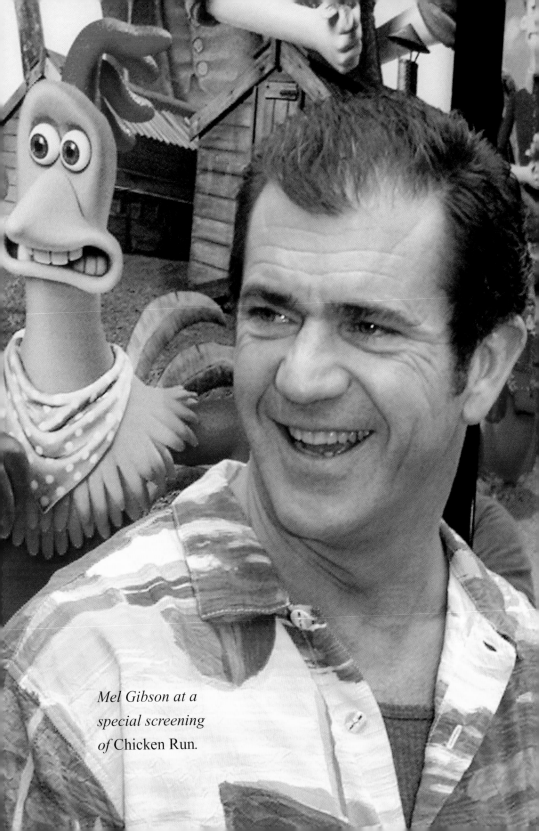

Mel Gibson at a special screening of Chicken Run.

In 2000, moviegoers enjoyed Gibson in both *What Women Want* and *The Patriot*. *What Women Want* is the story of a chauvinistic man who suddenly finds he can hear what women are thinking. *The Patriot* is the story of a widower with seven children who is drawn into the Revolutionary War.

Mel Gibson in Braveheart.

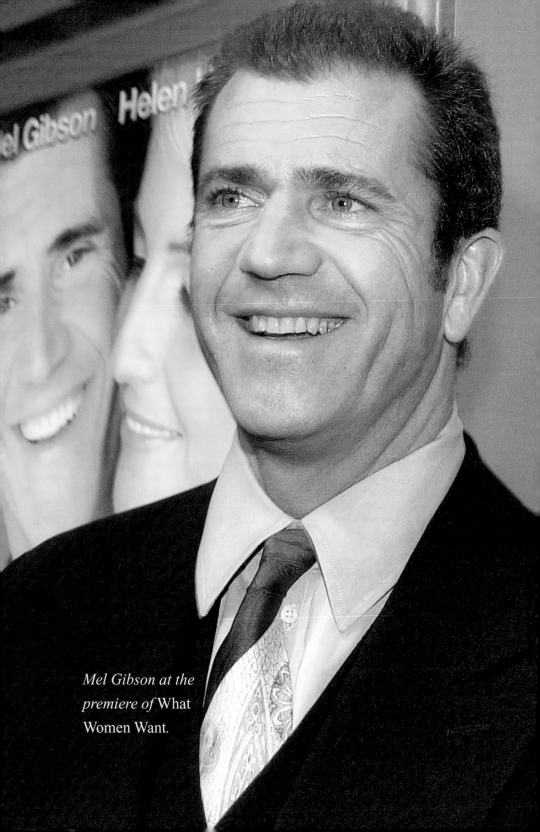

Mel Gibson at the premiere of What Women Want.

STILL A
HEARTTHROB

TODAY, THE GIBSON FAMILY DIVIDES
their time among homes in Connecticut,
California, and Australia (Gibson has both
United States and Australian citizenship). Gibson
has made it a point to take more time off between
movies to enjoy his family. He even refers to
Moore as "my Rock of Gibraltar, only prettier."

"Too many people go into marriage too
lightly," he told a reporter. "You've got to take it
seriously. Go in there wanting to make it last."

In Gibson's latest project he plays a farmer in
the movie *Signs*. Gibson's character discovers large
crop circles and other patterns on his farmland.
The movie was filmed at a private agricultural
school near Philadelphia, Pennsylvania.

To no one's surprise, the female students were
very excited at the prospect of Gibson visiting
their school. "Everyone knows he's coming," said
one student before filming began. "And all the girls
are waiting."

Mel Gibson in
We Were Soldiers.

GLOSSARY

Alcoholics Anonymous: an international organization that helps people overcome their alcohol problems.

chauvinist: a man who thinks men are superior to women, or a woman who thinks women are superior to men.

platonic: a close relationship that doesn't involve romantic love.

WEB SITES

Would you like to learn more about Mel Gibson? Please visit **www.abdopub.com** to find up-to-date Web site links about Mel Gibson and his film career. These links are routinely monitored and updated to provide the most current information available.

INDEX

A
Academy Award 52
Adelaide, Australia 22
Air America 44, 46
Alcoholics Anonymous 49
Asquith High School 15
Attack Force Z 28
Australia 14, 15, 20, 22, 24, 27, 28, 30, 32, 35, 38, 41, 42, 44, 58
Australian Film Institute 27, 32

B
Bayside, ME 4
Best Actor Award 27, 32
Bird on a Wire 44
Bligh, Captain William 35
Bounty 35
Bounty, The 35, 38
Braveheart 52

C
California 58
Chicken Run 54
Christian, Fletcher 35
Connecticut 58
Conspiracy Theory 54

D
Death of a Salesman 35
Disney 54

E
Egypt 30
England 15, 52

F
Ford, Harrison 36
Forever Young 49
Foster, Jodie 52

G
Gallipoli 28, 30, 32
Gallipoli, Ottoman Empire 30

Garner, James 52
Gibson, Anne 8, 46
Gibson, Christian 32, 58
Gibson, Edward 32, 58
Gibson, Hannah 30, 58
Gibson, Hutton 8, 10, 12, 14, 15, 41
Gibson, Louis 42, 58
Gibson, Mary 16, 58
Gibson, Milo 44, 58
Gibson, Tommy 54, 58
Gibson, William 36
Glover, Danny 42
Golden Globe Award 52

H
Hamlet 46, 49, 52
Hawn, Goldie 44
Hell's Angels 27
Henry IV 27
Hollywood, CA 4, 7, 35, 36, 42, 46
Hunt, Linda 7

I
Indonesia 32
Ireland 15
Istanbul, Turkey 30

J
Jeopardy 14

K
Keaton, Diane 36

L
Laos 44
Lethal Weapon 42
Lethal Weapon 2 44
Lethal Weapon 3 49
Lethal Weapon 4 54

M
Mad Max 24, 27, 32, 38
Mad Max: Beyond Thunderdome 38, 41
Man Without a Face, The 4, 50, 52
Maverick 52

Miller, Dr. George 24
Moore, Robyn 7, 22, 28, 30, 38, 44, 58
Mrs. Soffel 36, 38
Murtaugh, Roger 42
Mutiny on the Bounty 35

N
National Institute of Dramatic Arts 16, 19, 20, 24
Neill, Sam 28
New York 8
New York Central Railroad 8, 10, 12
New York, NY 8
New Zealand 28, 30

O
Oedipus Rex 27
Oscar 52

P
Patriot, The 56
Payback 54
Peekskill, NY 8
People 41
Philadelphia, PA 58
Philippines 32
Pocahontas 54
Punishment 28

R
Ransom 54
Revolutionary War 56
Riggs, Marty 42, 44, 49
River, The 36, 38
Road Warrior, The 32
Roberts, Julia 54
Rome, Italy 15
Romeo & Juliet 20
Russell, Kurt 44
Russo, René 7, 54

S
Scotland 15, 52
Shakespeare, William 46

Shannahan, Bill 24
Signs 58
Smith, John 54
South Australian Theatre Company 20, 22
Spacek, Sissy 36
St. Leo's College 15
Summer City 20, 24
Sydney, Australia 15, 16, 35

T
Tahiti 35
Taiwan 28
Tennessee 36
Tequila Sunrise 44
Thailand 44
Tim 27
Toronto, Canada 36
Turkey 30
Turner, Tina 41

U
United States 12, 27, 28, 58
University of New South Wales 16

V
Vatican 15
Victoria, Australia 35
Vietnam 12, 15

W
Waiting for Godot 20
Wallace, William 52
Warner Bros. 49
Wayne, John 36
Weaver, Sigourney 32
Weir, Peter 28, 32
What Women Want 56
World War I 30
World War II 8

Y
Year of Living Dangerously, The 32

Z
Zeffirelli, Franco 46